A true story from the Bible

MOSES
and the
VERY BiG
RESCUE

·WRITTEN BY·
Tim Thornborough

·IllUSTRATED BY·
Jennifer Davison

Moses and the Very Big Rescue © The Good Book Company, 2020. Reprinted 2021, 2022, 2024.
Words by Tim Thornborough. Illustrations by Jennifer Davison. Design and art direction by André Parker.

thegoodbook.com • thegoodbook.co.uk • thegoodbook.com.au • thegoodbook.co.nz • thegoodbook.co.in

ISBN: 9781784985578 | JOB-007604 | Printed in India

You've probably learned to count upwards:

1, 2, 3, 4....

But when they fire a rocket into space or when something AMAZING is about to happen, we sometimes count downwards:

3, 2, 1...

In this true story from the Bible, God counts down to the Very Big Rescue of his people.

God's people had a

VERY BIG PROBLEM.

Pharaoh was the king of Egypt.
He had made them his slaves.

They worked all day in the hot sun to
make bricks for Pharaoh's buildings.

So they cried out to the Lord for help.

And God heard them, and planned a

VERY BiG RESCUE!

God told Moses, "Go to Pharaoh and tell him to

"LET MY PEOPLE GO."

God said, "I will do amazing things to show him who is really the King of the world. Pharaoh will know that I am the one true God."

So Moses went.

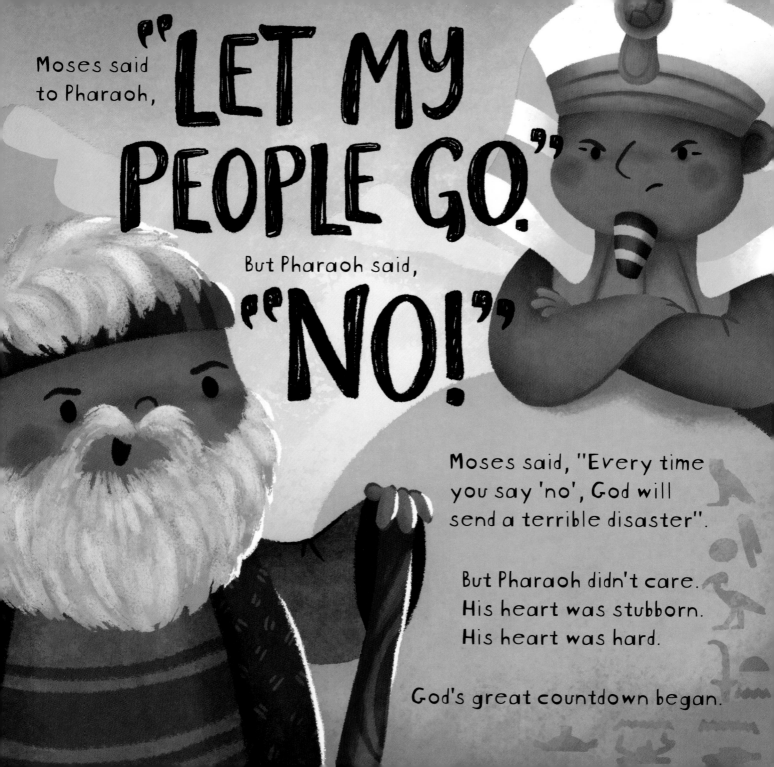

Moses said to Pharaoh, **"LET MY PEOPLE GO."**

But Pharaoh said, **"NO!"**

Moses said, "Every time you say 'no', God will send a terrible disaster".

But Pharaoh didn't care. His heart was stubborn. His heart was hard.

God's great countdown began.

10 Moses held out his staff over the great River Nile, and it turned to blood.

But Pharaoh was stubborn.
His heart was hard.
He would not let them go.

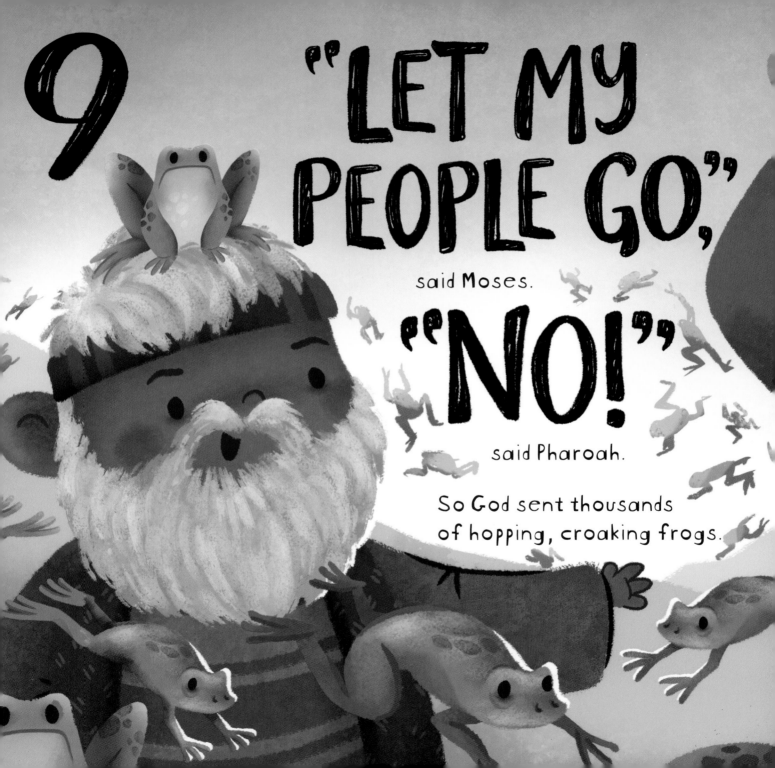

8 "LET MY PEOPLE GO",

said Moses. But Pharaoh said,

"NO!"

And God sent millions of whining, itching gnats.

But Pharaoh was stubborn. His heart was hard.

6 "LET MY PEOPLE GO,"
said Moses.

"NO!"
said Pharaoh.

So God sent a sickness on the cattle and sheep.

But Pharaoh was stubborn. The Lord had hardened his heart.

5 "LET MY PEOPLE GO,"

said Moses.

"NO!"

said Pharaoh.

So God sent a plague of painful, purple pus-filled boils.

4 "LET MY PEOPLE GO,"

said Moses.

"NO!"

said Pharaoh.

So God sent huge, hurtling, horrible hailstones.

3 "LET MY PEOPLE GO"

said Moses.

"NO!"

said Pharaoh.

So God sent
swarms of noisy,
hungry locusts.

2 "LET MY PEOPLE GO"

said Moses.

"NO! NO! NO!"

said Pharaoh.

So God sent a deep, inky darkness,
so no one could see anything.

But Pharaoh was stubborn.
The Lord had hardened his heart.

"LET MY PEOPLE GO,"

said Moses.

"NO!"

said Pharaoh.

And Moses had a sad heart as he left Pharaoh because he knew that the last plague would be terrible...

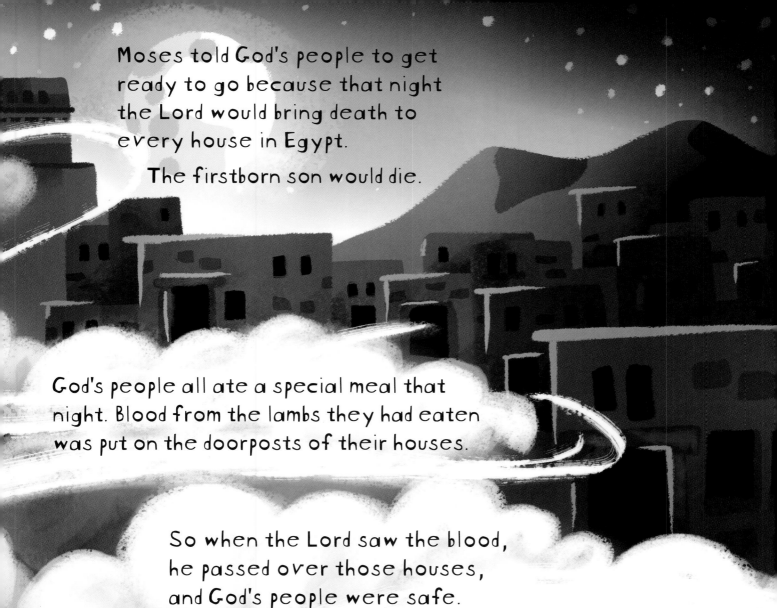

Moses told God's people to get ready to go because that night the Lord would bring death to every house in Egypt.

The firstborn son would die.

God's people all ate a special meal that night. Blood from the lambs they had eaten was put on the doorposts of their houses.

So when the Lord saw the blood, he passed over those houses, and God's people were safe.

But in every other house in Egypt, there was death and great sadness.

But Pharaoh was stubborn.
His heart was hard.

And he chased after God's
people with his army and
his chariots.

"They are trapped by the sea,"
thought Pharaoh.
"I will destroy them all."

God had reached the end of his countdown:
10, 9, 8, 7, 6, 5, 4, 3, 2, 1...

ZERO

Moses held up his staff,
and the sea parted
before him.

All God's people walked through
the sea and got safely to the
other side.

But when Pharaoh and his horses and chariots tried to follow...

...the sea rushed back and they were drowned.

God had rescued his people from Egypt.

Moses and the people danced
and sang a song together:

"There is no one like you, Lord.
You do great miracles and wonders.
You keep your promises
and save your people.
Praise the Lord!"